AF585102

Australian States *and Territories*

VICTORIA

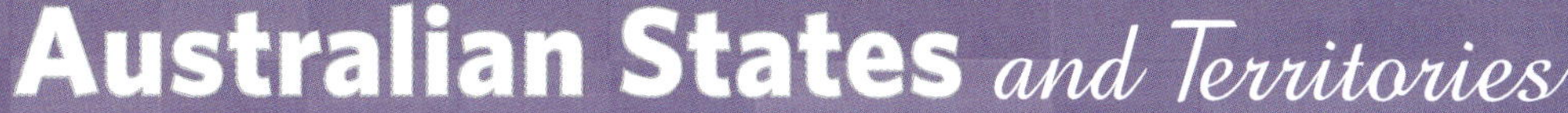

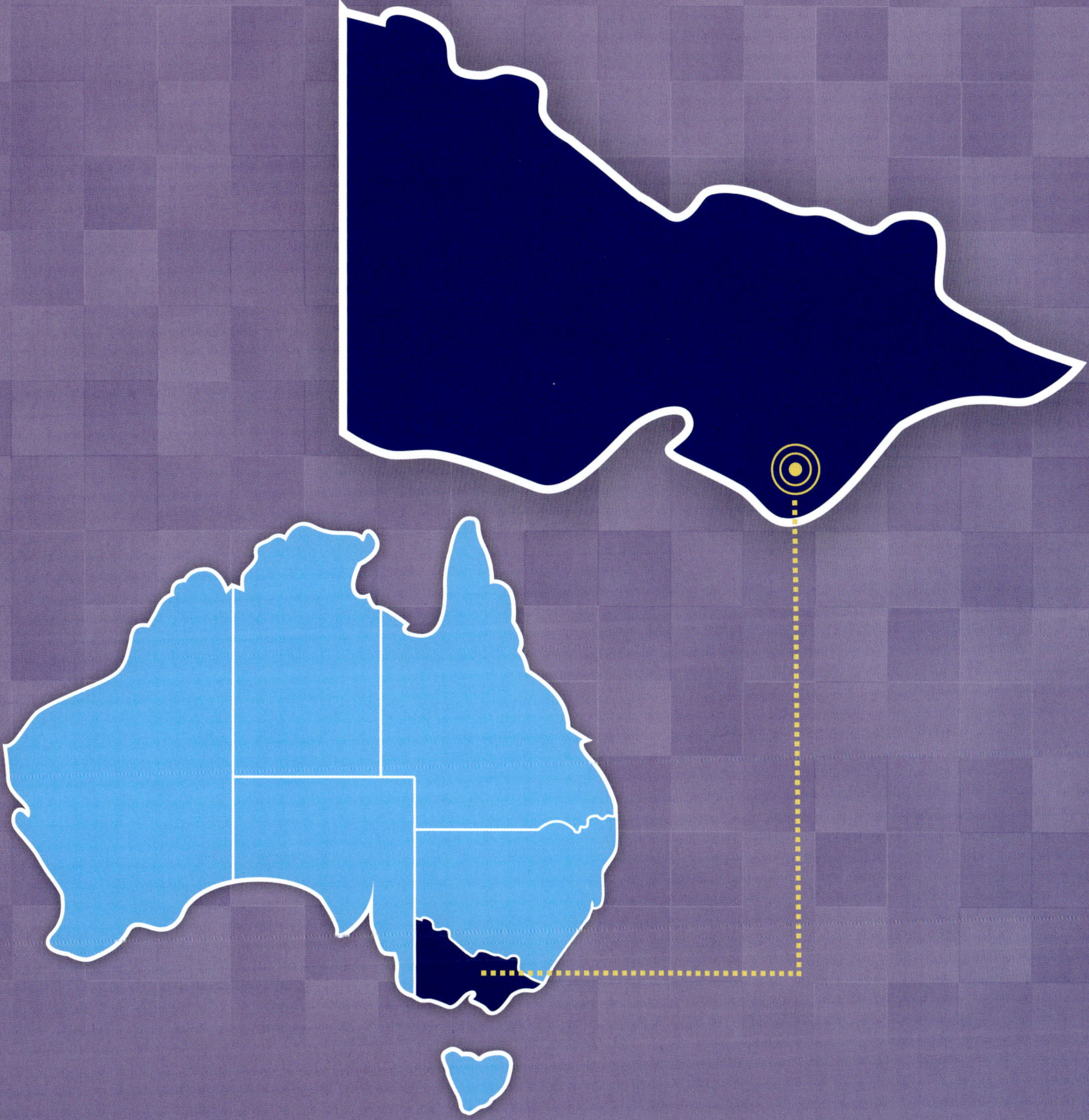

Linsie Tan

REDBACK publishing

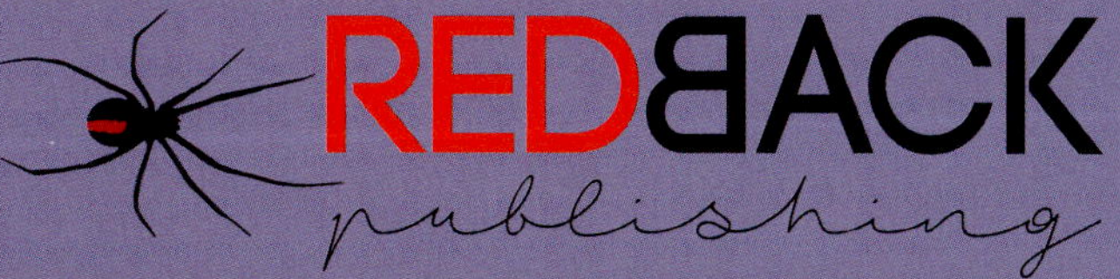

Redback Publishing
PO Box 357 Frenchs Forest NSW 2086
Australia

ISBN 978-0-9946247-6-5

First published 2017
Reprinted 2018

Author: Linsie Tan
Editor: Jane Hinchey
Original illustrations © Redback Publishing 2017
Originated by Redback Publishing
Printed and bound in China by Leo Paper

Acknowledgements
We would like to thank the following for permission to reproduce photographs: Neale Cousland / Shutterstock.com, tirin, stevage, State Library of Queensland, FiledIMAGE / Shutterstock.com, ingehogenbijl / Shutterstock.com, Steve Lagreca / Shutterstock.com, Featureflash Photo Agency / Shutterstock.com, tristan tan / Shutterstock.com, Mitchell Library, State Library of New South Wales, Neale Cousland / Shutterstock.com, Brendan Howard / Shutterstock.com, Tuangtong Soraprasert / Shutterstock.com, Squiresy92 including elements from Sodacan, Denver Faingold, Le Dawn Studios, photographer and State Library of Victoria.

Every effort has been made to contact copyright holders of any material reproduced in this book. Any omissions will be rectified in subsequent printings if notice is given to the publisher.

Cataloguing-in-Publication details are available from the National Library of Australia

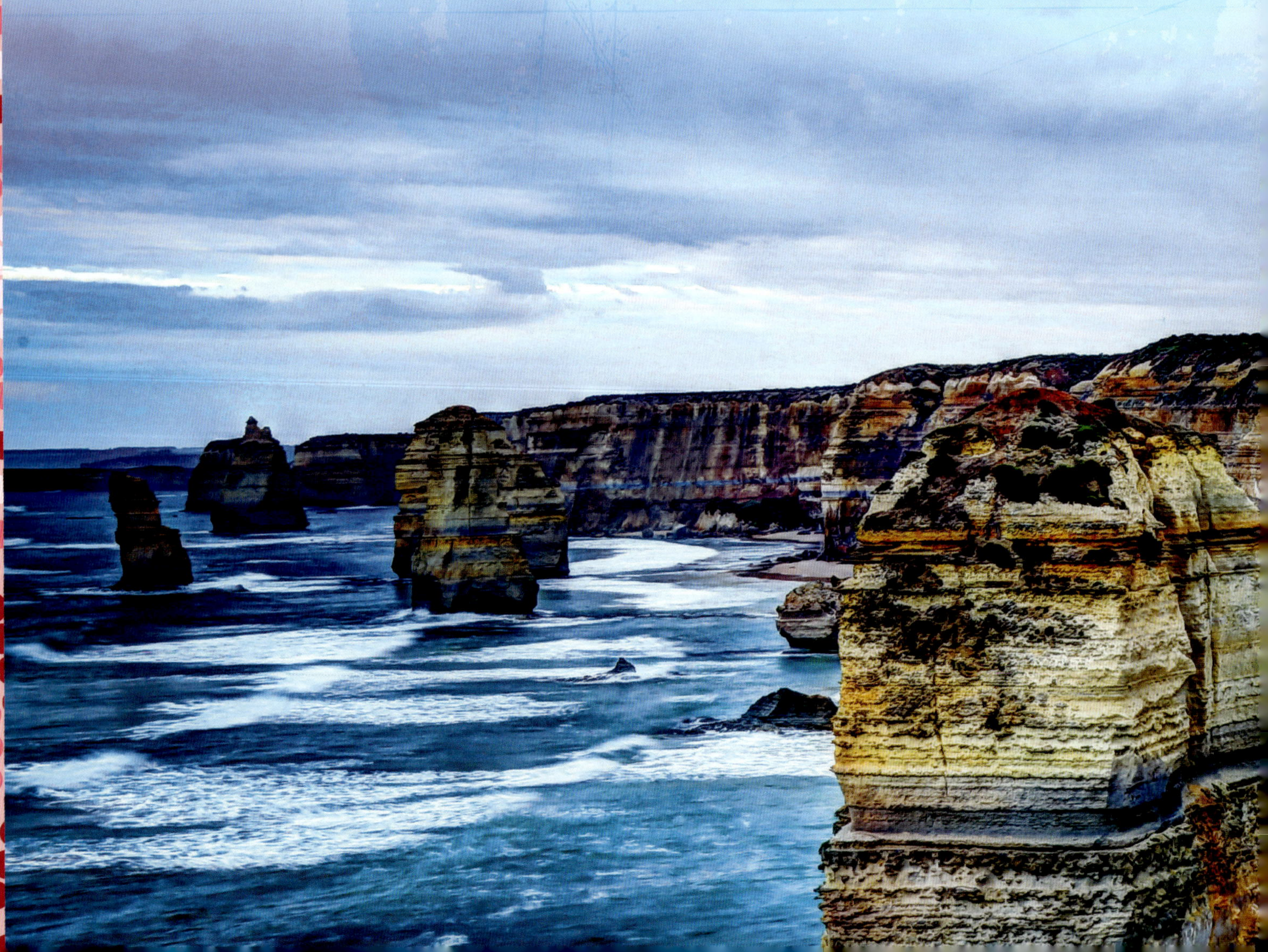

CONTENTS

Some words are shown in red, **like this**.
You can find out what they mean by
looking in the glossary.

Geography of Victoria

Victoria is the second smallest state of Australia, but it has the second largest state population. The capital city is Melbourne on the Yarra River. The nearest country is New Zealand, which is to the east across the Tasman Sea.

The Southern Uplands

The Southern Uplands are near the coast south of Melbourne. Wilson's Promontory, which is the most southerly point on the Australian mainland, is in this region. It was recorded by George Bass on his journey around the southeast coast of Australia in 1797.

The Southern Plains

The Southern Plains are where Victoria's brown coal deposits are found. Fertile soils and dependable water supply provide good pastures for sheep and cattle.

The Murray Basin Plains

The Murray Basin Plains are in the north of the state and are important for wheat growing. They include the driest parts of Victoria. The rivers in this region mostly flow north into the larger Murray River.

The Central Highlands

Mount Bogong is the highest mountain in Victoria at 1,986 metres high. It is part of the Australian Alps in the Central Highlands of Victoria. The Alps have their own alpine ecology and are a tourist attraction for hiking and skiing.

The Dandenong Ranges

The low hills of the Dandenong Ranges are home to a wide range of wildlife. Picnic areas and walking trails make the whole region a popular destination.

Islands of Victoria

The Phillip Island Nature Parks are not far from Melbourne. The island is famous for the nightly 'Penguin Parade' as little penguins emerge from the sea and waddle back to their burrows. There is also a motor-racing circuit on the island. Other islands include Gabo Island and French Island. They are both important havens for wildlife.

FAST FACTS

The three major rivers of Victoria:

- **The Murray River - 2,530 km (forms most of Victoria's boundary with NSW)**
- **The Goulburn River - 583 km**
- **The Glenelg River - 454 km**

Population

Victoria's population is about 6 million people, which is around 25% of Australia's total population. 75% of all Victoria's workforce lives in Melbourne.

PREDICT THE POPULATION

Draw a graph using these figures. Can you use the graph to work out what the population of Victoria might be in the year 2051?

YEAR	1851	1901	1951	2001	2051
POPULATION of Victoria	97,500	1,210,000	2,300,000	4,790,000	?

Climate

The Great Dividing Range runs across Victoria from east to west, dividing the state into two areas and affecting the climate in each. The areas south of the mountains are temperate. North of the mountains the weather is more dry and hot.

Regional Centres

Large regional centres in Victoria are at Ballarat, Bendigo, Geelong, Shepparton, Mildura, Traralgon, Warrnambool and Wodonga.

FAST FACTS

- Highest recorded temperature: 48.8 °C at Hopetoun Airport in 2009.
- Lowest recorded temperature: -11.7 °C at Falls Creek in 1970.

WORD FILE

temperate - having a mild climate

Aboriginal History of Victoria

Aboriginal people have lived in Australia for at least 60,000 years. They developed complex societies and ways of life, and their culture depends on having strong spiritual connections to the land.

Ancient History of Victoria

8,000 years ago Victoria and Tasmania were connected by land, which allowed Aboriginal people to migrate back and forth. There are over 30,000 Aboriginal archaeological sites in Victoria, showing the remains of ancient ways of life. There are human burials, used shells, scarred trees, stone tools and fish traps.

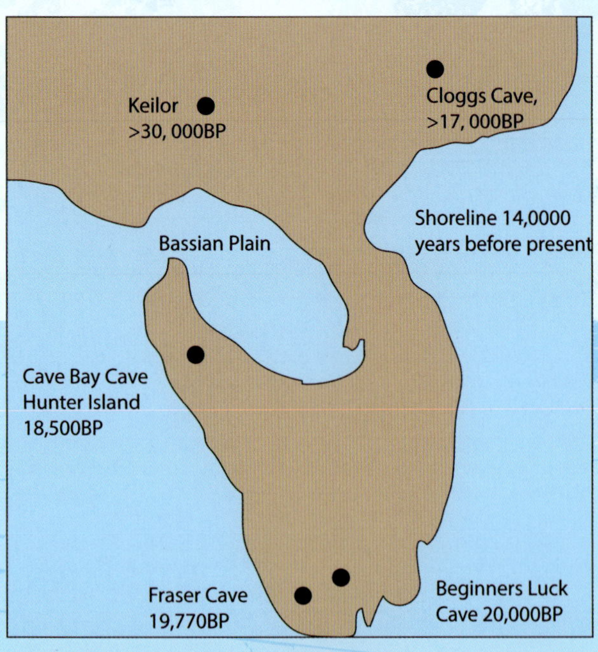

What Food Did They Eat?

Knowledge of the seasons and animal habits were very important for finding food. The range of foods Aboriginal people ate depended on the region of Victoria where they lived. In the Melbourne area Aboriginal people hunted kangaroos, possums, bandicoots, koalas, echidnas, wombats and birds. They caught fish and eels and collected oysters. They also enjoyed many vegetables and fruits, including the 'daisy yam'. In the plains areas the range of food was not as wide because of the lack of water during droughts. Along rivers and valleys there was plenty of food for hunting, fishing and gathering.

Aboriginal Australian man outside shelter, 1866, N. J Caire.

What Sort of Housing Did They Build?

In the Melbourne area and along inland rivers Aboriginal people built shelters made from mud or clay, bark and wood. In the plains areas they used temporary campsites as they had to move around to hunt for game or find water.

The Grampians National Park

The Grampians has the largest number of rock art sites in the southern area of Australia. The art includes red ochre hand stencils, spirit figures and symbols. Archaeologists used charcoal from ancient campsites to work out that Aboriginal people have lived in the Grampians for at least 22,000 years

FAST FACTS

The winters in Victoria can be very cold so the Aboriginal people wore long fur cloaks made from the animals they hunted.

Aboriginal Nations and Clans in Victoria

There are many different Aboriginal nations, each with its own lands and cultural traditions. A nation is defined by its connection to its land and by its language. Groups within a nation may also have their own dialects.

1859

FAST FACTS

The 5 Aboriginal language groups of central southern Victoria

Bun Wurrung	Mornington Peninsula and north to the Dandenongs
Woi Wurrung	Yarra River to Mt Macedon
Wada Wurrung	Bellarine Peninsula and Otway Ranges
Djadja Wurrung	Loddon and Avoca Rivers, Bendigo
Daung Wurrung	Mount Buller to Kyneton

European Settlers and the Aboriginal Nations

The Aboriginal nations had strong relationships with the land, and this caused conflict between them and the European settlers. Cattle and sheep replaced native food animals on the land, and settlers colonised areas for themselves that had been in traditional ownership for thousands of years.

Most Aboriginal people living in the Melbourne area were moved onto a government mission beside the Yarra River in 1837. In 1847, many Aboriginal people in the Port Philip District died after catching influenza.

William Cooper, Aboriginal Leader, 1861 - 1941

On behalf of the Melbourne Aboriginal community, William Cooper set up a petition in the 1930s seeking voting and land rights. The idea for **NAIDOC Week** grew out of Cooper's wish to have a national **Aborigines' Day**.

Aboriginal Australians camped in the bush near the Yarra River, ca. 1859 - 1863, Richard Daintree

WORD FILE

colonise - to settle in a new land and impose a new culture on the people living there
traditional ownership - the Aboriginal land ownership system in existence before the arrival of Europeans
dialects - different forms of the one language

Colonial History of Victoria

Victoria was originally part of New South Wales and was known as the Port Phillip District. In 1851, Victoria became a separate colony with its own government.

Timeline
The Exploration of Victoria

- **1770** – Captain James Cook saw the coast of Terra Australis for the first time at Point Hicks.
- **1797** – George Bass sailed around the coast of Victoria and decided that Tasmania must be a separate island. Before this, most people thought it was connected to the mainland.
- **1802** – Lieutenant Murray claimed Port Phillip for Britain. Soon after, Matthew Flinders arrived to survey the area.
- **1803** – A small group of convicts was sent to settle in Port Phillip near Sorrento.
- **1824** – Explorers Hamilton Hume and William Hovell travelled south through New South Wales and crossed the Murray River into Victoria.
- **1830** – Charles Sturt explored the Murray River in his search for grazing land.
- **1834** – Edward Henty set up the first permanent settlement in Victoria at Portland Bay.
- **1835** – John Batman chose the site for Melbourne.
- **1860** – Robert Burke and William Wills left Melbourne to explore a route to the north of Australia.

BURKE & WILLS
150 YEARS CROSSING AUSTRALIA 2010
AUSTRALIA 60c

The Port Phillip District

From 1840, the settlers of the Port Phillip District on the Yarra River had many concerns about the way the colonial government in Sydney was treating them. There were complaints about the lack of a bridge over the Yarra River, bad roads and a poor water supply. In 1851, the Port Phillip District became the colony of Victoria and was no longer under the control of New South Wales. Gold was discovered in the same year, resulting in a massive increase in population and wealth for Victoria.

Melbourne (Port Phillip), 1841, John Adamson

The 'Wild White Man'

Convict William Buckley escaped from the settlement near Sorrento in1803 and lived with the local Wathaurung people until he was found by John Batman in 1835. He had forgotten his own language and was identified by a tattoo of his initials on his arm.

Who Were the Settlers in the Early Colony?

Convicts

Convicts were never sent directly to Port Phillip from England. Most of them were moved there from New South Wales or Van Diemen's Land.

Free Settlers

Since Melbourne was settled mostly by free settlers and not by convicts, as in Sydney, the European inhabitants wanted to keep their new colony free from prisoners transported from England. However, there were not many other sources of labour for farming and building.

John Batman

Settlers from Van Diemen's Land (now Tasmania) attempted to buy land from the Aboriginal people in the Port Phillip area in 1835. One of these settlers was John Batman. He signed a treaty with the local Aboriginal people and took ownership of the land. He then decided on a site for the town of Melbourne. Governor Bourke in New South Wales heard about this and declared the treaty and Batman's settlement unlawful.

TIME TRAVELLER

Imagine you are one of the Aboriginal people making a treaty with John Batman to sell your land to him. How do you feel about your land? How does he view your land? What do you think of him?

Settlers' Houses

The settlers lived in many different types of housing, depending on how wealthy they were and whether they had convicts or other labourers to help build their houses.

Bark huts - A wooden frame covered in sheets of bark.
Wattle and Daub - A wooden frame plastered with a mixture of soil, clay and manure.
Brick houses - Convicts made bricks from clay.
Stone - Stonemasons built houses and public buildings from local sandstone.

People were supposed to build their houses in neat rows in the new town of Melbourne, but many ignored this rule.

WORD FILE

Terra Australis - the European name for Australia before it became a British colony in 1788
treaty - an official agreement between nations

The Gold Rush and the Eureka Stockade

The gold rush started in 1851. It was a major economic event in Victoria's history. People came from around the world to look for gold. The wealth created by gold mining turned small country villages into large towns. In the ten years after 1851, Victoria produced one third of the world's gold.

The Gold Mining Towns

Ararat - In 1857, a group of Chinese miners discovered gold.
Ballarat - The site of the Eureka Stockade.
Bendigo - Two women found gold in 1851.
Castlemaine - In 1852, had a population of 30,000 and was the richest goldfield in the world.

Other gold rush towns included Beechworth, Maryborough, Jamieson, Maldon and Creswick.

Chinese Goldminers

Thousands of Chinese came to the Victorian goldfields. When the Victorian government started charging them a tax for arriving on ships, some Chinese miners overcame this by sailing to South Australia instead and walking to the Victorian goldfields.

FAST FACTS

The largest gold nugget found in Victoria weighed 76.5 kg. It was discovered near Ballarat in 1869 and was called the Welcome Stranger.

Gold mining, Chinese encampment, Guildford near Castlemaine circa 1861

Eureka Stockade

In 1854, goldminers in Ballarat, angry at high licence fees imposed by the government, surrounded themselves with a wooden stockade and fought a battle with soldiers and police. Many people on both sides died and the remaining goldminers were arrested. The result of the battle was that the licence fee was reduced. This victory encouraged others to strive for voting rights and freedom from unjust laws. The goldminers' Eureka flag has become a well-known symbol across Australia.

Eureka Flag

TIME TRAVELLER

Imagine you are one of the miners inside the Eureka Stockade. How do you feel about the battle which is about to start?

Eureka Stockade, ca. 1890 -.1900, B. Ireland

The Gold Rush and Business

The people who came to Victoria to join the gold rush needed food, clothing, equipment and other goods and services. Small businesses started in every gold mining town to serve the miners and provide them with everything they needed. Builders and tradesmen benefitted from the building boom and banking expanded to look after the miners' wealth.

The gold rush was responsible for Victoria's economic growth during the mid to late 1800s. The expansion of the railway system to country areas was partly a result of demand from mining communities for easy access to Melbourne.

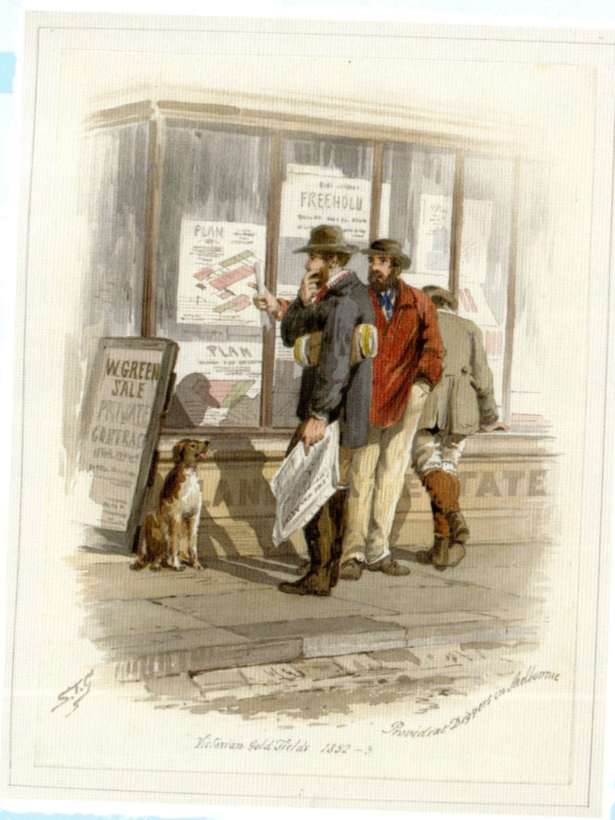

Provident diggers in Melbourne, 1869,S. T Gill

Transport in Victoria

Pre-Colonial Transport

The first methods of transport used by Aboriginal people in Australia were walking and paddling canoes. Canoes were made of bark or from hollowed out logs, and they were used for fishing and to cross rivers and harbours. 'Canoe trees' along the Murray River have large scars where bark was peeled from them to make canoes. The Melbourne Museum has an example of a bark canoe in its collection.

Aboriginal people travelled to locate food sources, to attend ceremonies and to trade with other groups of people. They had well-known routes which they used for generations and part of one of these trails is now along the Princes Highway starting at Sale.

Aboriginal canoe tree, Upper Murray, ca. 1910 - 1930, Dorothy Susan

Horses and Coaches

The first settlers walked, rode horses or travelled in carriages. For those who could afford them, Cobb & Co coaches were a popular way to travel longer distances before a railway existed. The first Cobb & Co country journey was to the gold fields in Bendigo in 1854.

Trains

In 1854, Australia's first steam train ran on a track between Flinders Street and Port Melbourne. Railways made the transport of produce fast and simple, and they contributed to the economic development of the state. The line to Geelong opened in 1857, to Ballarat via Geelong in 1862, to Bendigo in 1862, to Echuca in 1864 and to Wodonga in 1873. Melbourne was the first Australian city to electrify its suburban railway network in 1919.

Buses

Horse drawn buses were used by the people of Melbourne before other forms of mass transport were available. One of these could carry up to 14 people.

TIME TRAVELLER

Imagine you are a passenger on a Cobb & Co coach in 1854. What are you wearing? What is the journey to Bendigo like compared to today in a car? Is it comfortable?

Victorian Railways electric tram,1906

Trams

Melbourne is renowned for its trams. While other capital cities in Australia have stopped using their tram services, Melbourne has developed its trams so that they are a continuing feature of its city and culture. The original trams pulled on tracks by horses were replaced in 1885 by a cable system. The first electric trams began running in 1889.

Shipping at Port Melbourne, ca.1870

River Transport

Echuca had a large wharf on the Murray River for loading the paddle steamers that carried wool and agricultural products to Melbourne.

Shipping Ports and River Transport

The shipping ports of colonial Victoria expanded during the gold rush to cater both for the thousands of immigrants coming to seek their fortune, and to handle the exports of the growing agricultural industries. The principal shipping ports today are at Melbourne, Geelong and Portland. Melbourne has Australia's largest container port.

Paddle-steamers at wharf, Echuca, 1866, G. H. Kendall.

FAST FACTS

AIRPORTS, ROADS & BRIDGES

- Tullamarine Airport in Melbourne is the major airport in Victoria. There are also many regional airports.
- The Hawthorn Bridge over the Yarra River was first built in 1861 and modified in later years. It is now the oldest metal truss bridge in Australia.

WORD FILE

container port - a place where ships load large metal containers full of cargo

Industry in Victoria

The Victorian economy makes up about 23% of the total for Australia. Unlike other larger states, Victoria does not depend as much on mining for its state income. Victoria's main increase in jobs in recent years has been in the service industries rather than in mining, agriculture or manufacturing.

Mining

Brown coal, gold, mineral sands and metal ores such as bauxite, for aluminium, are all mined in Victoria.

Oil and Gas

Victoria's oil and gas production is located in the waters of Bass Strait. Mining takes place from offshore platforms, or oil rigs, and workers have to travel to them by boat or helicopter.

Electricity

Brown coal from the Latrobe Valley still supplies over 80% of the power source for electricity production in Victoria. The government is looking at ways to increase its use of renewable energy sources.

FAST FACTS

Exports from Victoria:

- Wool
- Wheat
- Aluminium
- Dairy foods
- Processed meats

Most of Victoria's exports go to China, USA, New Zealand, Japan and Saudi Arabia.

Manufacturing and Business

1. The financial services industry in Victoria employs 12% of all workers in the state. It includes businesses that cover banking, insurance, share trading and accounting.
2. The manufacturing industry produces many items for local and international use, including automotive parts, electronics and machinery, chemicals and plastics, pharmaceuticals, fabricated metals and clothing.
3. International education is one of Victoria's growing industries.

Tourism Industry

The scenic and varied countryside of Victoria makes it popular with tourists. Attractions include pioneer themed villages, natural sites, stunning coastlines and historic buildings.

Sovereign Hill Pioneer Village

This is a recreated mining village, situated near Ballarat, where visitors can experience the lifestyle of a gold rush town of the 1850s. It is an outdoor, living museum.

Pioneer Settlement, Swan Hill

Another recreated historic village, located near the banks of the Murray River. It shows visitors the way of life of the Mallee region's pioneers.

Wineries

The Grampians wine region is the birthplace of Australia's sparkling wine industry. There are many historic wineries to visit in this area.

WORD FILE

service industry - work that assists customers rather than making or building things

Agriculture in Victoria

Victoria's main agricultural products are dairy, meat, fruit, vegetables, wheat and sheep's wool.

Wheat and Other Grains

Grains are grown across Victoria's northwestern area in the Loddon-Mallee and Wimmera regions. Victorian grain exports are around 14% of Australia's total. Half the wheat grown in Victoria is used in the state, while the rest is exported.

Dairy Farming

Dairy farming occurs in the north, southwest and Gippsland regions. Victoria provides about 85% of Australia's dairy exports. Only about 10% of milk produced is used locally in liquid form. The rest is made into other dairy products.

Meat

Sheep and beef cattle are raised in the Grampians, Loddon, Mallee, Barwon and Gippsland areas, as well as in parts of central Victoria. Goat farming is one of Victoria's growth industries.

FAST FACTS

The Victorian government has policies to control the farming of animals. They cover:

- food safety
- animal welfare
- biosecurity
- protecting the environment

Fruit and Vegetables

A large proportion of Victoria's fruit and vegetables is grown in the Mornington Peninsula and the Cardinia and Yarra Ranges Shires. Grape growing occurs around Mildura, the Yarra Valley and Mornington Peninsula. Victoria is also a significant producer of tomatoes, lettuces and mushrooms.

Timber

Victoria produces timber from its eight million hectares of forests. This includes 223,000 hectares of forest plantations, which are a renewable resource.

Wool

Most of the sheep farming for wool occurs in the western regions of Victoria. China is the largest export market for Victorian wool.

Grapes and Wine

Victoria produces about one third of all Australia's grapes, and is the third largest wine-producing state. Wine is produced by both small family businesses as well as very large companies. The industry faces a constant battle against insect pests such as aphids and fruit flies.

Seafood

Trout, barramundi, yabbies and abalone are raised in farms in Victoria's rivers, and commercial fishing harvests fish from the open ocean. All fishing in Victoria is controlled by the need for licences, setting of catch limits and allowing only permitted equipment. To protect the sustainability of the seafood resource, the Victorian government will phase out the use of commercial fishing nets in Port Phillip Bay by 2022.

QUICK QUIZ

What crop, plant or animal is grown by farmers so that we can have these things in our homes?

- Toast
- Hot-cross buns
- Woollen blankets
- Meat pies
- Yogurt
- Wooden toy box

WORD FILE

biosecurity - controlling plants, insects and animals that are harmful

Environment and Sustainability in Victoria

Many parts of the natural environment have been destroyed since the first small European settlement in Victoria in 1803. Sustainable practices for agriculture and industry require a balance between using the land and waterways for development and keeping areas as regions of natural beauty. The protection of endangered plants and animals is also important.

Mackenzie Falls, Grampians National Park, Australia

National Parks

Because of its varied geography, Victoria is very popular with tourists. 14% of Victoria is wilderness, parks or reserves. The national parks are managed so that their beauty can be enjoyed in an environmentally sustainable way, and so that endangered plants and animals are not further threatened. Over one million hectares of Victoria's national parks provide a catchment area for water used in agriculture and for drinking.

RESOURCES	HOW WE CAN LOOK AFTER THEM
SOIL	Correct use of fertilisers and avoiding soil erosion
FORESTS	Using plantations for timber
WATER	Keep water supplies unpolluted
NATIVE PLANTS	Avoid complete clearing of areas for pastures
NATIVE ANIMALS	Keep some areas of natural bushland for food and shelter
AIR QUALITY	Avoid polluting the air through poor industrial practices

Bush Fires

Aboriginal people used fire to encourage grass to grow so that hunting was easier. European settlers had little knowledge about how to control bushfires and they experienced many devastating fires. The worst bushfires in Australia's recorded history were the Black Saturday bushfires in 2009.

Firefighters are employed by the Victorian government. Along with the volunteers of the Country Fire Authority, they not only fight bushfires but are also involved in fire prevention activities, such as planned burning.

Renewable Energy

Renewable energy comes from solar power, wind power, water power and biofuels. Victoria is seeking to increase its use of renewable energy sources for generating electricity.
Water Power - Uses the movement of the sea and rivers
Wind Power - Uses windmills
Solar Power - Uses the sun
Bioenergy - Uses plant or animal matter

Protecting Native Plants and Animals

Endangered animals in Victoria are affected by habitat loss, introduced species, infectious diseases, fire and climate change. Some of these animals are:

- Blue whale
- Brush-tailed rock wallaby
- Mountain pygmy possum
- Southern bent-wing bat
- Southern right whale

Brush-tailed rock wallaby

Waterwatch Victoria

This is a program that encourages volunteers to check the health of the state's waterways. Some of the environmental problems they encounter are algae, floods, poisons running into rivers, and development that damages waterways.

WORD FILE

sustainability - ability of the environment to be used without being destroyed
plantations - farms used to grow one product, such as trees for timber

Government of Victoria

Before colonisation, Australian Aboriginal nations throughout Victoria governed according to their own laws.

Timeline Before Federation

1770 Captain James Cook explored the coast of eastern Australia and claimed the land for Britain.

1788 Governor Phillip was the highest authority in the whole colony.

Charles La Trobe

1839 Lieutenant Governor La Trobe was appointed to govern the Port Phillip District, which was still a part of New South Wales.

1851 The colony of Victoria separated from New South Wales. Men who owned property could vote for two thirds of the members of the Legislative Council and Lieutenant Governor La Trobe chose the rest.

1854 Victoria's constitution was created.

1856 The first fully elected Legislative Council and Legislative Assembly met. There were now two houses of parliament, as there are today.

Parliament House Victoria, ca. 1900 - 1949

FAST FACTS

'Terra nullius' is Latin for 'land that nobody owns'. The British government used this idea to allow them to claim land in Victoria.

Woman voting at Wangaratta, 1970

Local Government

Victoria has 79 local government councils. They are elected by people in the area and look after local services such as suburban streets, libraries, garbage collection and parks.

The first local government area created in Victoria was the Town of Melbourne in 1842, followed by Geelong in 1849.

The Victorian Parliament Today

There are two sections, or houses, in the Victorian parliament. This is called a bicameral system. All members are elected by voters. Laws are made after both houses debate and vote on them.

1. The Legislative Assembly - this is also called the Lower House. It has 88 members.
2. The Legislative Council - this is also called the Upper House. It has 40 members.

Timeline After Federation

1901 Federation meant Victoria became a separate state with its own government.

1908 Women could vote. Victoria was the last state to give women the right to vote.

1962 All Aboriginal Australians could vote in state and federal elections.

1924 Women could stand for election in Victoria.

1950 People no longer needed to own property to be allowed to vote for the Legislative Council.

1973 People over the age of 18 could vote.

1979 First women elected to the Legislative Council.

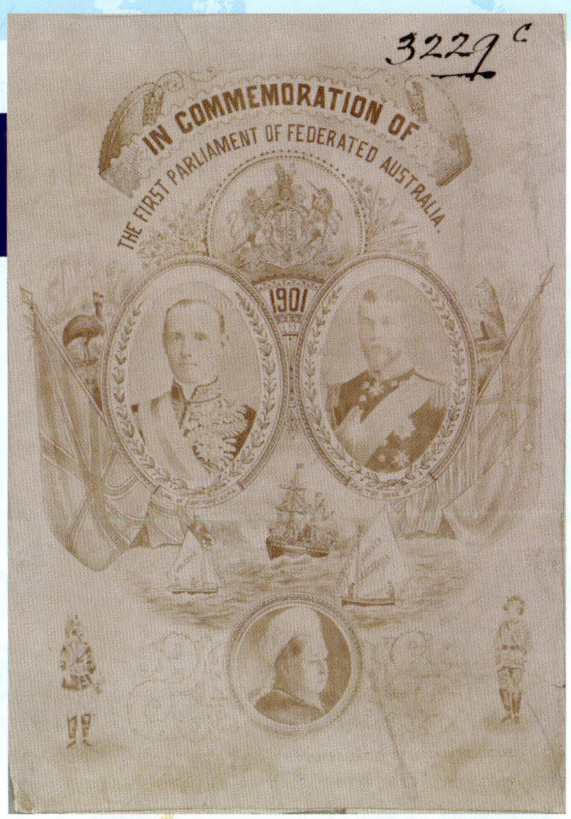

WORD FILE

constitution - a set of rules and ideals by which governments operate

bicameral - a government having two houses or sections

Notable People from Victoria

Government

Robert Menzies (1894 - 1978) was born in Jeparit. He was Australia's longest serving Prime Minister and a founding member of the Liberal Party. In 1939, at the beginning of the Second World War, he gave a famous speech declaring that Australia was at war with Germany.

Sport

Shane Warne (1969 -) was born in Upper Ferntree Gully. He is possibly the best bowler in the history of Australian cricket.

Lionel Rose (1948 - 2011) was born at Jackson's Track near Labertouche. He was the first Aboriginal Australian to win a world boxing title in the bantamweight division. He also had a successful singing career in the country music industry. There is a memorial statue of him at Warragul.

MAKE YOUR OWN LIST

Who are three people you think are important in your family, school or suburb?

What makes a person memorable?

Science

Macfarlane Burnet (1899 - 1985) was born in Traralgon. He was awarded the Nobel Prize in 1960 for his research into immunology. In the same year, he became the first person to be named as Australian of the Year. Modern influenza vaccines are still made using the results of his discoveries.

Religion

Saint Mary Mackillop (1842 - 1909) was born in Fitzroy. In 2010, she became Australia's first and only Saint. She founded the Sisters of St Joseph at a very young age, and spent her life teaching and setting up refuges for people in distress.

Entertainment

Nellie Melba (1861 - 1931) was born in Richmond. She was the first Australian opera singer to gain international fame. Her real name was Helen Mitchell but she chose the name 'Melba' because she came from Melbourne.

Authors

John Marsden (1950 -) was born in Melbourne. His books have won many awards and will be found in nearly every school and public library across Australia. 'Tomorrow When the War Began' was made into a movie and released in 2012.

Andy Griffiths (1961 -) was born in Melbourne. He is a very popular author of children's books, including the bestselling Treehouse series. His humorous books attract all sorts of readers, and often include cartoons by Terry Denton.

Art

Arthur Boyd (1920 - 1999) was born in Murrumbeena. His large tapestry hangs in the Great Hall of Australia's Parliament House in Canberra.

Bushranger

Ned Kelly (1855 - 1880) was born in Beveridge. Whether Ned Kelly was just a criminal or a local hero, he has become a source of inspiration for films and novels. He killed police officers but claimed he and his family had been treated badly by them. His home-made armour is a recognisable image in many works of art based on his life, particularly the series painted by Sidney Nolan.

Immigration to Victoria

People have come from around the world to live and work in Victoria. Their cultures and skills have contributed to the social diversity of the state.

Timeline - Immigration in Victoria

- **At least 60,000 years ago**: The ancestors of the Australian Aboriginal people arrived from the north and spread throughout the country.
- **Before 1851**: 90,000 migrants from Britain sailed to Victoria and took up jobs as labourers and servants.
- **After 1851**: The gold rush attracted over 600,000 immigrants to Victoria.
- **1901**: The White Australia Policy restricted the arrival of 'non-white' people.
- **1947**: Beginning of the post World War II surge in migrant numbers from Europe.
- **1975**: Vietnamese refugees started arriving after fleeing South Vietnam.

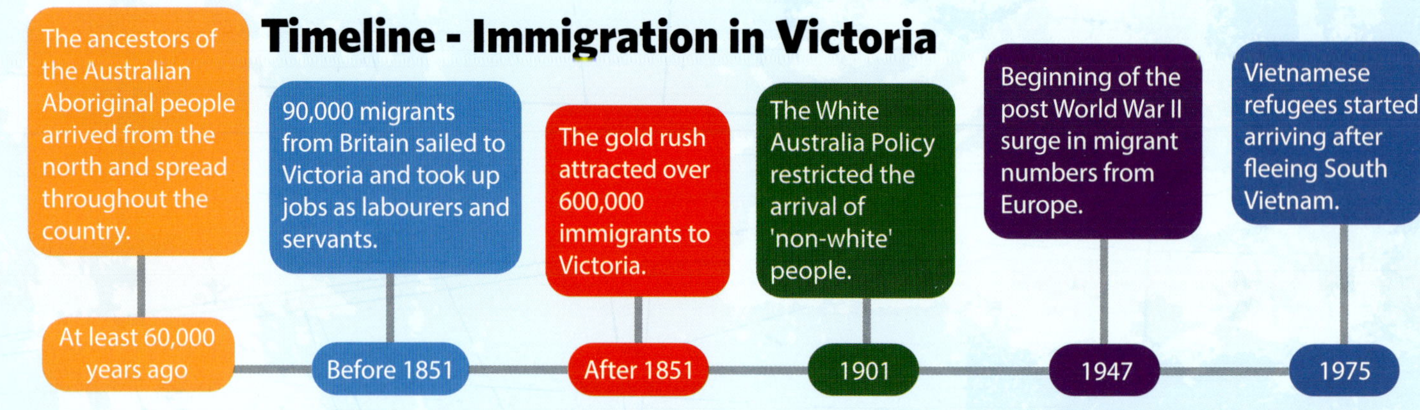

The Bonegilla Migrant Camp

In 1947, the Victorian government opened the Bonegilla Centre in Wodonga to house new migrants, most of whom were from Europe. The living conditions were simple, and there was little privacy. Bonegilla was closed in 1971. Block 19 is the only building still remaining and it is now a museum.

DID YOU KNOW?

In the 1850s there were so many immigrants arriving that they had to live in a tent city on the Yarra River bank south of Melbourne.

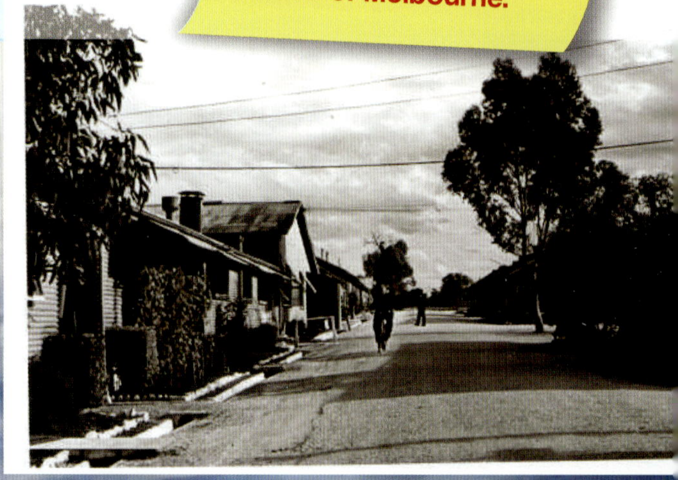

Bonegilla Migrant Camp block 19, 1984

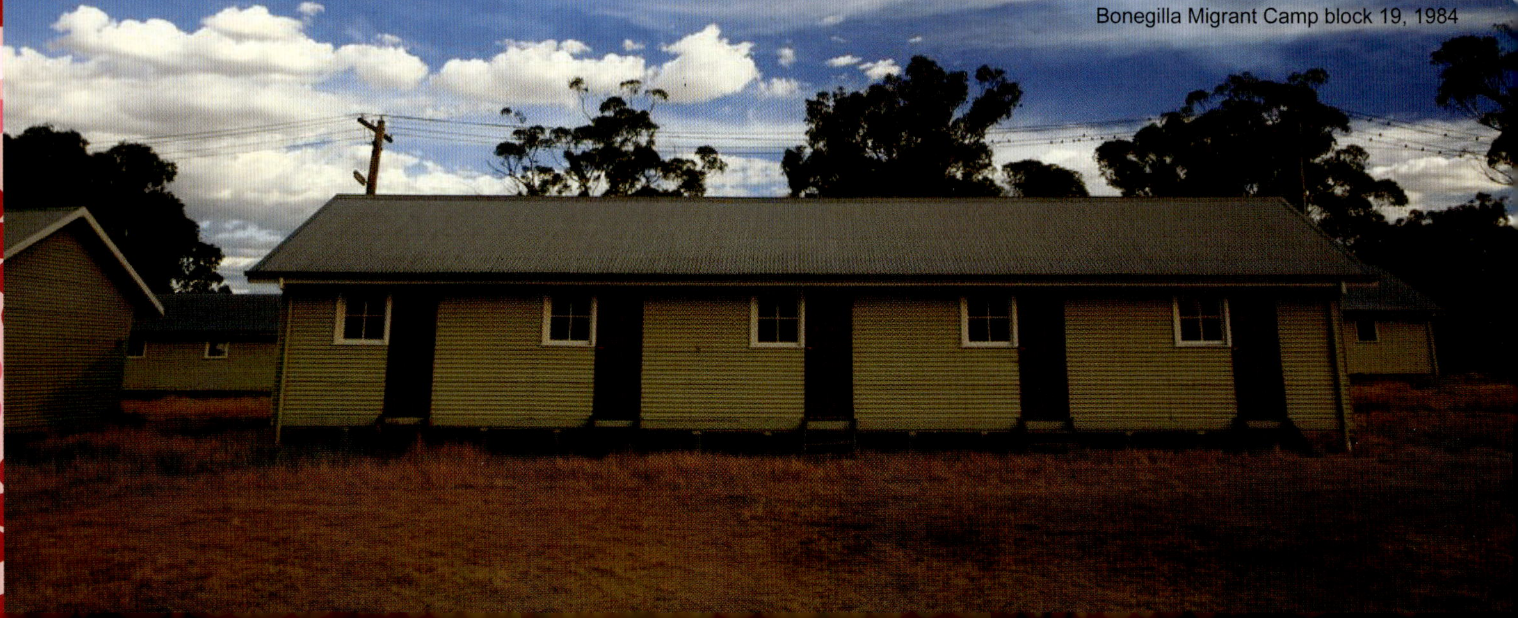

Britain

Until recently, immigration from Britain was supported by a number of government schemes. In 2011, they were the third largest migrant group in Victoria.

Greeks and Italians

Italians formed a local branch of the cultural group, the Dante Alighieri Society, in Melbourne in 1896. This was the first branch outside Italy. Sicily and Calabria were the main places from which Italians chose to emigrate to Victoria. Greek people also came in large numbers after the Second World War, giving Melbourne one of the largest populations of Greek people outside Greece. The Greeks and Italians who made Melbourne their home have contributed greatly to the city. Most came by ship to Melbourne, with the last migrant ship arriving in 1977.

Emigration in search of a husband, 1833

Asia

The White Australia Policy restricted all Asian immigration until it was abolished in 1966. Now Asian countries top the list of nations providing immigrants to Victoria. These countries include India, China, Sri Lanka and Burma. Amongst the Indian migrants there is a high proportion of trained people, with about 42% working in professional roles.

FAST FACTS

AFTER THE GOLD RUSH 80% of the people who stayed in Victoria had come from Britain. 10% of the people who stayed had come from Germany, America and China.

The Middle East

The Lebanese Civil War, 1975 - 1990, led to more than 40,000 refugees coming to Australia, some ending up in Melbourne. Refugees from Afghanistan and Iraq are the most recent arrivals to Victoria from the Middle East. The Afghani community in Victoria is the second largest in Australia.

OTHER COUNTRIES

Migrants to Victoria have come from many other countries apart from the ones listed above. How many can you name?

Javanese and Fijian women and children refugees in Melbourne, ca. 1942

Major Sites in Victoria

These sites include buildings, structures and natural features. They are important for their beauty, rarity and historic connections.

Royal Exhibition Building, Melbourne, ca. 1885 - 1890

Royal Exhibition Building

Built in 1880 for the World's Fair, this is one of the last exhibition style buildings from the era still left in the world. The surrounding gardens have also been preserved

The Twelve Apostles

These spectacular rock pillars in the sea off the Great Ocean Road are a major tourist attraction.

The Great Ocean Road

Follows the coastline from Geelong to the South Australian border and offers outstanding scenery.

FAST FACTS

There is one World Heritage Site in Victoria: The Royal Exhibition Building and Carlton Gardens in Melbourne

National Parks

The Alpine National Park - the largest in Victoria at 646,000 hectares
Great Otway National Park - features ancient forests and waterways
Grampians National Park - known for its Aboriginal rock art

Rippon Lea House and Garden

Designed by Joseph Reed in 1868, this Italianate style mansion in Elsternwick is now partly a house museum. Visitors can see a way of life that used the most advanced technology of its time, and compare this with houses today.

Melbourne Cricket Ground

The MCG is the world's largest cricket stadium. In 1877, the first game of Test cricket was played at the MCG between Australia and England. In 1956, it was the main stadium for the Olympic Games.

Glenrowan Heritage Precinct

An eight hectare site that encloses many locations of the main events in the life of bushranger, Ned Kelly.

Eureka Stockade Gardens

This park commemorates the Eureka Stockade of 1854, when goldminers clashed with police and soldiers over licence fees for miners. The gold deposits they were mining are still underneath the park. There are no relics of the stockade left above ground.

Eureka Stockade Memorial Gardens, Ballarat, 1953

Flags, Symbols, Emblems and Special Days of Victoria

People living in Victoria use flags, symbols and special days to show their connection to their community.

Victorian State Flag

In 1865, Victoria became the first colony to have its own flag. The flag was originally created for use on ships but it has now become a symbol for all of Victoria. The Union Jack reminds us of Great Britain, and the five stars represent the Southern Cross. In 1877, the imperial crown was added.

Australian Aboriginal Flag

The Aboriginal Flag was first flown in 1971. It was designed by Elder Harold Thomas.

Yellow disc - the sun and yellow ochre

Red - the land

Black - the Aboriginal people of Australia

RULES FOR FLYING THESE FLAGS

- Don't fly more than one on the same pole
- Don't fly them in the dark
- Raise the flag to the top of the pole before lowering it to half-mast
- Treat these flags with respect

Special Days

Australia Day - On 26th January each year, Australians commemorate the founding of the first British colony in Terra Australis at Sydney Cove in 1788.

ANZAC Day - Ceremonies and marches for ANZAC Day are held all around the state on 25th April each year. The largest march in the state is in Melbourne.

NAIDOC Week - A week in July each year to celebrate the history, culture and achievements of Aboriginal and Torres Strait Islander peoples. Various communities and local and Victorian governments organise events around the state for NAIDOC Week.

Melbourne Cup Holiday - Held on the first Tuesday in November, this public holiday is for the horse race that is held at Flemington Racecourse. People all around Australia stop whatever they are doing at 3pm on that day each year to find out which horse will be the winner.

Moomba Festival - Five days of events and a large parade in Melbourne each March attract many locals and tourists.

Symbols of Victoria

Floral Emblem - Common pink heath
Animal Emblem - Leadbeater's possum
Bird Emblem - Helmeted honeyeater
Fish Emblem - Weedy seadragon
Gemstone Emblem - Gold

The Coat of Arms

This is a symbol of Victoria.
Five Stars - represent the Southern Cross
Woman on the Right - represents Peace and therefore holds an olive branch
Woman on the Left - represents Prosperity and holds a Horn of Plenty
Motto - Peace and Prosperity

Make Your Own Coat of Arms

Design a Coat of Arms for your family, suburb or sport group, etc.

- Use symbols that everyone will know
- Your own Coat of Arms could include drawings or pictures to tell the history of the group
- Think about where to use your Coat of Arms
- Where have you seen the Victorian Coat of Arms used?

WORD FILE

Elder - a respected Aboriginal person who is a custodian of traditional knowledge
half-mast - flying a flag halfway up the pole as a mark of respect when a community leader dies
Horn of Plenty - a symbol for wealth and abundance

How to Find Out More
Primary and Secondary Sources

There are many ways to find out more about Victoria. You can do this using both primary and secondary sources. Websites can have a mixture of both types of sources on them.

Primary Sources

- **Interviews** - when people say what they have seen
- **Letters** - when the writer was the person experiencing the event
- **Newspapers** - when the facts are presented
- **Photos** - when they have not been altered
- **Maps**
- **Old Items & Antiques**
- **News on Television** - when it shows pictures of a real event or a person saying what they have seen
- **School Newsletters** - when they list names or dates of events
- **Videos on Youtube or Facebook** - when they show an event and have not been altered

Secondary Sources

- **Letters** - when the writer is retelling the facts that someone else told them
- **Newspapers** - when the story is told by someone who retells the facts that someone else told them
- **Photos** - when the photo has been altered
- **Songs, Poems, Stories**
- **News on Television** - when it is reported by a journalist who did not experience the event

Fun Activities Using Sources

- Look up your own suburb in the Victorian Hansard and find out what politicians say about it. Go to www.parliament.vic.gov.au and click on 'Hansard search'.
- Find old newspapers at your local library. Use these to look at pictures of areas you know and to see how they have changed over time.

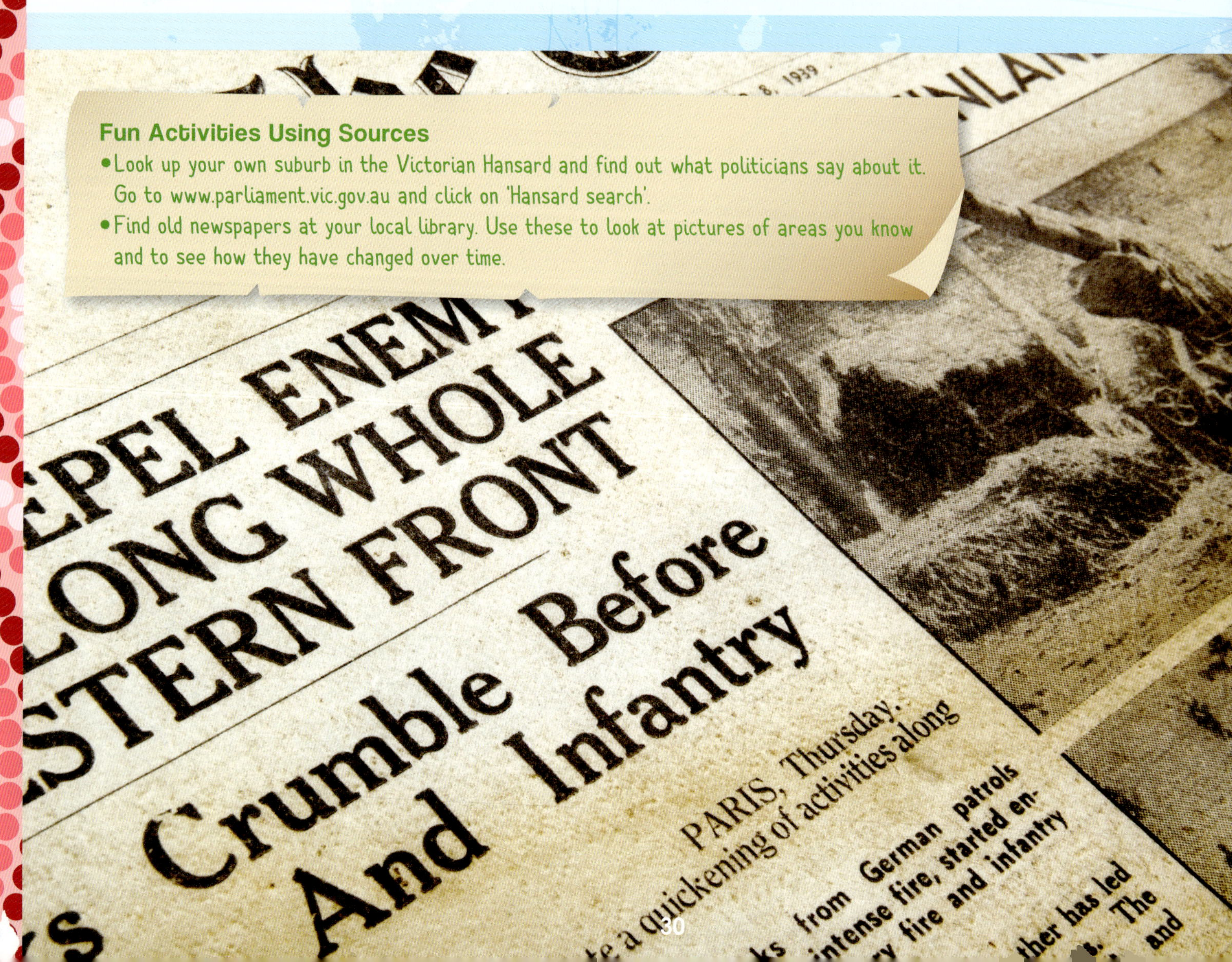

Museums

Visit museums to look at primary sources. For instance, you could look for examples of clothing that rich and poor people wore.

Major museums in Victoria

- Gum San Chinese Heritage Centre, Ararat
- Pioneer Settlement, Swan Hill
- Sovereign Hill, Ballarat
- Golden Dragon Museum, Bendigo
- Melbourne Museum, Carlton
- Bunjilaka Aboriginal Cultural Centre, Carlton
- Brambuk Centre, Halls Gap

Your Own Family and Friends

Primary sources do not always have to be about famous people. Interviews with your family and friends are important too. Your grandmother might recall what your suburb used to be like. Friends can share stories about coming to live in Victoria either from other states or from a country overseas.

Websites

- The Brambuk Centre website explores the Aboriginal cultural history of the Grampians region www.brambuk.com.au
- Find out about the work being done to preserve the health of Victoria's water resources www.vic.waterwatch.org.au
- All about Victoria, including history and tourist sites www.visitvictoria.com
- Many interesting pages on all aspects of Melbourne's past and present www.emelbourne.net.au
- The first newspaper in Victoria was the 'Melbourne Advertiser' which began in 1838. Its early issues were written by hand. Find images of the pages at, www.trove.nla.gov.au
- Find the Victorian government Hansard at, www.parliament.vic.gov.au/hansard

Glossary

bicameral - a government having two houses or sections
biosecurity - controlling plants, insects and animals that are harmful
colonise - to settle in a new land and impose a new culture on the people living there
constitution - a set of rules and ideals by which governments operate
container port - a place where ships load large metal containers full of cargo
dialects - different forms of the one language
Elder - a respected Aboriginal person who is a custodian of traditional knowledge
half-mast - flying a flag halfway up the pole as a mark of respect when a community leader dies
Horn of Plenty - a symbol for wealth and abundance
plantations - farms used to grow one product, such as trees for timber
service industry - work that assists customers rather than making or building things
sustainability - ability of the environment to be used without being destroyed
temperate - having a mild climate
Terra Australis - the European name for Australia before it became a British colony in 1788
traditional ownership - the Aboriginal land ownership system in existence before the arrival of Europeans
treaty - an official agreement between nations

Index

www.redbackpublishing.com.au